Silence

Kyle D. Jones

We are supposed to embrace silence.
How have we come to escape it?

– Kyle D. Jones

Acknowledgements

Char.

Tables of Consciousness

DESTINY'S CHILD - NO SUCH
THING AS THE FUTURE - MORE,
MORE, MORE - HOW COULD YOU
- IDEAS ARE NOT REALITY - I
AM THE BODY - EVERYBODY
WANTS TO BE SOMEBODY -
TRAPPED IN CONSCIOUSNESS -
NEW CELLS HAVE FORMED -
THERE IS NO PERSON -
DISCOVER WHO YOU ARE -
EVERYTHING IS THE SAME
THING - NOTHING MATTERS -
MARILYN MONROE - AMERICA -
333 - THE NORM - LIVING IN
DENIAL - EARTH - WHAT AM I
DOING HERE? - DEATHLESS

SOULS - WE FEAR DEATH -
FOOTBALL FIELD OF
PERCEPTION - NO ONE - FAST
LIFE LIVING - EMPTINESS IS
WHOLENESS - BE REAL -
PARENTAL EXPECTATIONS - BE
A SUCCESS - BRAINWASHED -
THE ILLUSION - JOIN THE
ILLUMINATI - NORMAL -
CLOCKS AND CALENDARS -
MATERIALISM - THIS SILLY
GAME OF ESCAPISM - THE
ILLUSION OF COMFORTABILTY -
YOU THINK YOU KNOW

Prologue

Before the evolution of man, there was silence—only the sounds of nature existed. There were no cars, no planes, no music, and no vocalized forms of communication. Prior to the past 100,000 years, there was eternal silence.

What has happened to this silence? It is still here. However, we have become addicted to noise, as silence brings up the unanswered questions continuing to ponder at the back of our mind from childhood.

This book will bring these unanswered questions to surface. If you read with an open heart, it will also bring clarity into your experience. There is no longer a need to participate in the world of escapism and run away from silence. The time to expand human consciousness for the evolution of our species has come.

DESTINY'S CHILD

The child is told what reality is before his or her mind has evolved to inquire oneself; and as a result, society is filled with a bunch of obedient children accepting false information as reality, living life in the world while empty inside.

NO SUCH THING AS THE FUTURE

We waste our life preparing for the future, not realizing the only way to be happy is being immersed in each moment.

The act of going to first grade, second grade, third grade, and so on is nonsense.

The act of setting a goal, accomplishing it, and setting another is nonsense, bullshit.

We live our lives in a time-based manner, never stopping to realize the concept of time is not real, that clocks were invented about five hundred years ago.

We live our lives in a time-based manner, never stopping to realize each moment is eternal; and that this eternality is what we waste our whole life searching for in future preparation.

MORE, MORE, MORE

The world exists because we are in denial to the truth of being here, existing now, so we go on attempting to make existence more than it is.

Since the evolution of man, we strived to reach the Golden Age. The Golden Age has come; and life is filled with objective manifestations not mandatory to exist.

Names, jobs, schools, clothes, and phones are not needed. These unnecessary states of being have derived from our unconscious desire to make existence more than it is.

The more we desire to make existence more than it is, the longer we will remain ignorant to what has always been, that which we are truly seeking through the world—silence.

HOW COULD YOU

How could you look up at the clouds and look up at the sky like you know what that is?

How could you look up at the Sun and look up at the Moon like you know what that is?

How could you look in the mirror, see that body, and act like you know what that is, who that is?

You do not know what shit is; all you know is that you are here, and there is nothing else to know except that.

IDEAS ARE NOT REALITY

There is no death. There is no person. There is no world. These are ideas!

Our species will not be free until we liberate our mind of ideas; until we realize ideas are not reality; and that reality will forever remain unknown.

I AM THE BODY

This *"I am the body"* idea that has been passed down from generation to generation is destroying us, as it is the root of all evil and wrongdoing in the world.

This *"I am the body"* idea has caused us to focus on physical differences, compete with each other, neglect love and only desire to have sex with each other; as we hate each other and in turn hate ourselves.

This *"I am the body"* idea has caused us to ignore the unification of all life, ignore the truth of who and what we are, as we are nothing more than the observer playing hide and seek beyond the realm of the senses.

The world is suffering because it believes the body is the ultimate level of aliveness; however, it is not alive at all. The Consciousness that came into being is alive. The Consciousness that manifested into the body is what we are.

EVERYBODY WANTS TO BE SOMEBODY

Everybody wants to be somebody; and nobody has taken time to realize their body is composed of a trillion cells, that beneath each cell resides nothing except empty space.

Everybody wants to be somebody; and nobody has taken time away from this timeless thing to realize their body only appears real to the human senses.

Everybody wants to be somebody; and because of this, the world is suffering, at war, believing accomplishments are the ultimate purpose of life.

Everybody wants to be somebody, giving their entire attention to the world of no bodies, completely ignorant to what is making the body appear— pure energy.

TRAPPED IN CONSCIOUSNESS

We are too trapped in our own consciousness to accept there is nowhere to go.

No matter how far our GPS takes us, there is nowhere to go. No matter how many goals we achieve or how much money we build up in our bank account, there is nowhere to go. We will still be trapped within the field of our individualized consciousness, which itself is whole.

Every person we talk to, every thought we think, every sound we hear, anything we touch, and anything experienced is within our own consciousness. There is nothing except *It*. Despite all the people and things perceptually experienced, we are limited to experiencing ourselves. We are trapped in our own consciousness.

NEW CELLS HAVE FORMED

Even science has proven our body is constantly changing and recycling. We do not have the same body we used as a means of experience weeks ago. New cells have formed and taken place of the old; yet, we still have this limited idea of being this person with this body.

When will we realize anything that changes is governed by something changeless? When will we realize anything visible to the human eye is governed by something that cannot be perceived? When will we realize the body is an effect to a higher cause?

THERE IS NO PERSON

Everyone believes they are a person; and that why the world is suffering. There is no such thing as a person; it is only a popular idea we believe in, a limitation we have placed upon ourselves.

DISCOVER WHO YOU ARE

The most important thing you can do as a being of light in the human uniform is discover who you are. When you do not know who you are, you feel the need to become who society conditions you to become.

The problem with that is society itself does not know who it is. Society has yet to see beyond the human. The president, priests, doctors, psychologists, and other social roles have limited their seeing to the mind and body.

However, life exists beyond the mind and body; as you are more than these qualities glorified by the collective. You are a being of light. You are God playing the human role; but until you discover this, you will continue to live in lack and limitation, accepting what you are told as reality without questioning.

EVERYTHING IS THE SAME THING

How could one car be better than another, one house be better than another, one person be better than another, one's life be better than another?

How could anything be better than another when all is the same thing expressing itself in multiplicity?

Everything is the same thing no matter its material appearance and unique energetic expression. No matter where we look, there is the same thing expressing itself in a different way; and none of the ways of individualized expression could be better than another.

NOTHING MATTERS

Nothing matters; it is only the mind that makes it seem like things matter.

How could anything matter when once death occurs all is forgotten?

How could anything matter when all is temporary?

It is only the mind that remembers, holds on to things, wants things to matter; it is only the mind that keeps us blind to what is real, the silence, that which is always there.

MARILYN MONROE

Does it matter who the president is or what form of government we choose to construct the society?

No matter how much change he or she brings about, it is still within the structuring of a system—the very system that limits the evolution of our species.

To have a president and a government is a reflection of us thinking power exists outside ourselves, that life exists outside ourselves, that the world is more than a figment of our imagination.

In truth, it does not matter who the president is or what form of government we choose to construct our society—or even if society existed— because life always makes a way.

AMERICA

We say the pledge of allegiance almost every day for nearly twelve years of our lives; not because that is what we are supposed to do, but because we are being conditioned to believe America and the pathway of chasing the American Dream is for the betterment of us. As a result, we go through life limiting our imagination to America, never expanding consciousness to seeing the greater extraordinariness of life.

Psychology has proved we do not identify with our name and body until the age of three.

We do not limit our imagination to being personal, in a body, until the age of three.

We do not seek love, peace, and happiness outside ourselves until the age of three.

How much longer are we going to resist what we were prior to three years of age? How much longer are we going to deny what remains beneath the ideas and conditioning we have accepted as real?

THE NORM

Once you realize you do not have to follow the norm, that you have a choice, you allow yourself to experience true happiness—not the fabricated form of happiness everyone shows once they leave the comforts of their home, entering the world of pretenders.

Once you realize you do not have to follow the norm, that you have a choice, you allow yourself to enjoy the fullness of the human experience without limitation; you realize this entire time, you were limitless.

LIVING IN DENIAL

Many people deny being born knowing nothing.

Many people deny their mind has been conditioned by social predispositions since birth; and their way of perceiving life is not real, but a learned behavior.

Many people live in the world while dead inside, intuitively feeling there is more to life.

EARTH

No soul can come to Earth without manifesting a body.

WHAT AM I DOING HERE?

"What am I doing here?" is the question we have asked since manifesting into form.

However, since we have yet to receive an answer, we have pushed this question to the back of our mind; and it is eating us alive.

War, greed, lust, fear, and any other condition of sort is a result of this question mark.

The reason we pick up our phones, watch television, and resist spending time alone is to avoid this question coming up in thought.

This question is unconsciously beating our ass, fucking us up, and it is through ignorance we have given it power over our mind.

Ironically, there is no answer to this question. We will never know what we are doing here or how we got here; and we will never know what life is.

The only reason we ask this question is because we know there is more to life than the sperm and egg theory.

The only reason we ask this question is because we know there is more than this body disguising what is really there.

There is no answer to this question, but until we realize the world has tried to answer it, we will continue to seek one through escapism.

DEATHLESS SOULS

We are deathless souls afraid of dying, doing anything to escape the thought of it.

WE FEAR DEATH

How could we fear death when we were
"*dead*" before we came into the world?

FOOTBALL FIELD OF PERCEPTION

Everything experienced is within your own mind. You never leave your individualized field of perception.

NO ONE

The problem with the world is no one knows who or what he or she is.

Everyone has settled for the limited self-perception the world has impressed upon their mind.

Everyone thinks they are their names, bodies, beliefs, and past experiences; but how could this be?

How could this be what originally came into the body with no name, no beliefs, and no experiences?

FAST LIFE LIVING

We are in our twenty-somethings, getting high and fast life living, never slowing down to see what we are getting ourselves into.

We are getting ourselves into a lifelong journey of mental enslavement.

Can we not see it? Can we not see we were born knowing nothing and now pretend to know something?

We could not pronounce our name until after two years of consciousness. We believe age exist as reality rather than being our measurement of shifts in consciousness. We think our name is the clearest representation of who we are instead of something we have become conscious of.

We are in our twenty-somethings, and our mental comfort zone is molding shut. This could be the last chance we have to start thinking for ourselves. If not, we will journey through this lifetime thinking thoughts of the world, living in limitation, dying on the inside while pretending on the outer. If not, we will have to wait until our last breath to realize we lived a lie rather than awakening now.

BE REAL

How real is the world?

How real is life?

When will we stop to ask these questions?

When will we stop accepting what others impress upon our mind and start to think for ourselves?

PARENTAL EXPECTATIONS

The second we are born, our parents have expectations. They say, "He is going to be this and that and this," attaching themselves to ideals having nothing to do with the soul coming into the body.

Once we grow older, we enter grade school, which is said to help us become successful, another idea meaning nothing except the power we give to it.

We spend our whole lives bound by the achiever's mind, which is nothing more than a conditioned behavior; a product of our initial desire to make our parents happy by fulfilling their expectations.

We spend our whole life looking, chasing, and searching, not knowing what we are searching for is at the center of our being; that since birth we have overlooked it, as making our parents happy and making a name for ourselves became our main focus.

BE A SUCCESS

Every little boy or girl strives to be a success, due to social and parental pressures, born into a system that thrives off of the illusional thing success is.

Is there such a thing as success or is it an idea derived from the human imagination, given power through the collective consciousness?

Is there such a thing as success or are we born into a society that conditions our mind to believe celebrities are better than the homeless?

What is all this striving to be, to become, to achieve and accomplish? When will one stop to realize this is one big mindgame, a bunch of innocent souls mindfucked; so distracted by the technology era they never make time to be still and realize they are perfect as they are now?

BRAINWASHED

We listen to our parents as if they know the answers; but they know nothing except what someone else has told them.

Our parents were born with an empty mind. They had no conception of words, ideas, or what life was during the time of their birth. In fact, anything they know now is a result of societal conditioning; and anything they say does not make them right, but brainwashed longer than we have been.

The concept of being a parent has impacted the order of society and has kept the society in order. There is a difference between bringing another manifestation of life into being and being a parent to that manifestation. The conditioned idea of being a parent brings about control, authority, and unawareness to the difference between doing love and being love.

"Honor thy mother and thy father" is not something Jesus said; but something that has come about through the political and monetary values of the organized religion formed around the story of Him.

The concept of being a parent is an illusion; and the longer the child is obedient, the longer he will live his life bound by the ideals of his or her parents and the society.

There are so many of us going through life setting out to achieve what our parents want for us rather than what our heart desires. There are so many of us that reach middle age and are miserable with our lives. We are nothing more than a bunch of automated machines, limiting our imagination to what our parents conditioned us to perceive as possible and the right thing to do.

THE ILLUSION

The illusion of society is we are conditioned to believe there is a purpose to life, that there is something to do, that societal accomplishments equate to happiness and fulfillment.

JOIN THE ILLUMINATI

We try to find ourselves in the world while we lose our soul.

We do not necessarily lose our soul, but become blinded by the world and forget it exists.

We forget the soul came into and will leave the body when it learns what it needs on this plane of existence.

We cannot find ourselves in the world because we are the thing that manifested into it, the thing that is always here—forever.

NORMAL

The world defines normal; but what is that?

What is anything except our concept of it?

Concepts control our lives. Concepts limit our experience. To conceptualize any individualized expression of reality limits that individualized expression.

To conceptualize the Sun as the Sun, and believe the Sun is shining, blinds us to the beauty of our solar system's center.

To conceptualize the Earth as the Earth, and believe we are living on Earth, blinds us to the beauty of floating in the middle of nowhere at 1,040 miles per hour.

To define normal and believe we cannot experience life beyond what has been

perceived as so, blinds us to the beauty
of existing.

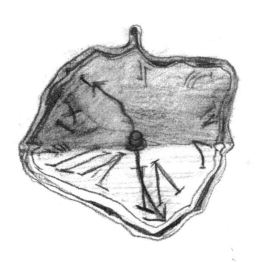

CLOCKS AND CALENDARS

We have clocks and calendars because we think time is real. We think time exists as an actuality instead of being our way of measuring shifts in consciousness.

MATERIALISM

We live in a world controlled by materialism, never realizing what the human mind conceptualizes as material is one percent matter—all else is empty space.

We live in a world controlled by materialism, never realizing beneath the forms of matter, molecules, particles and atoms reside nothing, not shit, not a damn thing.

We live in a world controlled by materialism, never realizing anything perceived on the material plane is projected from an immaterial plane, that nothing seen or acquired is real.

THIS SILLY GAME OF ESCAPISM

Do not be afraid of death. Be afraid of dying without knowing who you are. In fact, when you discover who you are, you discover immortality.

Though the body has an expiration date and is subject to change, there is something that forever lives and never changes. This is the immortal part of us, the only part of us, but we have limited ourselves to the mind and body.

When we realize the mind and body are an appearance of something else, that we are this something else, the fear of not living will neutralize the fear of dying; and it is the fear of dying that keeps the world playing its silly game of escapism.

THE ILLUSION OF COMFORTABILTY

A lot of people go their entire lives within their mental comfort zone. They think the same thoughts. They never expand consciousness beyond what their parents and teachers taught them.

YOU THINK YOU KNOW

If you think you know anything about life, you are lying to yourself.

Anything you know is something the world has taught you; and the world is not real.

SOURCES

Cain, Fraser. "How Fast Does the Earth Rotate?" *Universe Today*. N.p., 22 Dec. 2015. Web. 04 Feb. 2016.

"Clock Inventor - Who Invented Clock?" *Who Invented Clock?* History of Watches, n.d. Web. 07 Sept. 2016.

LeMind, Anna. "Top 10 Most Common Human Fears and Phobias." *Learning Mind*. N.p., 2014. Web. 17 Apr. 2016.

McLeod, Saul. "Id, Ego and Superego." Id Ego Superego. Simply Psychology, 2007. Web. 07 Jan. 2016

Smithsonian's National Museum of Natural History. "Introduction to Human Evolution | The Smithsonian Institution's Human Origins Program." *Introduction to Human Evolution | The Smithsonian Institution's Human Origins Program*. N.p., 2010. Web. 25 Feb. 2016.

Made in the USA
Lexington, KY
28 November 2017